Is the lost coin under the table?

Is the lost coin behind the lamp?

Is the lost coin in the corner?

Swish, swish.
Is the lost coin in a crack in the floor?

The woman was so happy she counts
the silver coins. 1-2-3-4-5-6-7-8-9-10.
" Be happy," she says.
" I have found my lost coin."